How Do Animals See?

Albatros

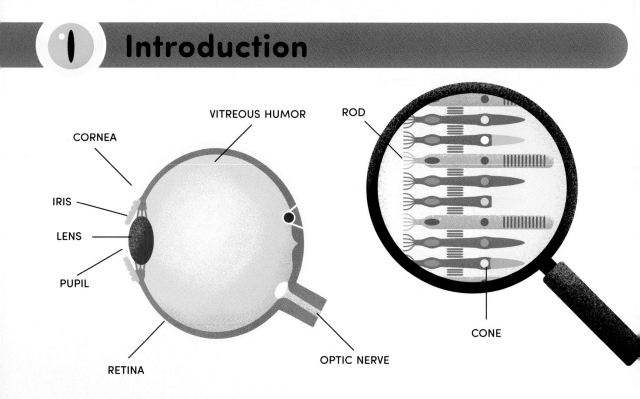

CORNEA

VITREOUS HUMOR

ROD

IRIS

LENS

PUPIL

RETINA

OPTIC NERVE

CONE

For many species, especially **vertebrates** and various **arthropods**, the eyes are one of the most distinctive organs. Through them, animals perceive a great deal of information from the external environment: **light, colors, movement, and space**. For some animals, sight is the most important sense. Did you know that human eyes perceive up to 90% of all external environment information? The **chamber of the eye**, which you have as well, is a kind of **light detector** that consist of several layers. The outer covering is called the **cornea**. Behind the cornea is the **iris**, at the center of which is an opening called the **pupil**. It manages the intensity of the light that enters the eye. The **lens** focuses light through the **vitreous humor**, which supports the **retina**.

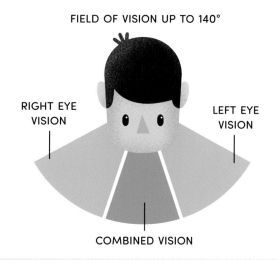

FIELD OF VISION UP TO 140°

RIGHT EYE VISION

LEFT EYE VISION

COMBINED VISION

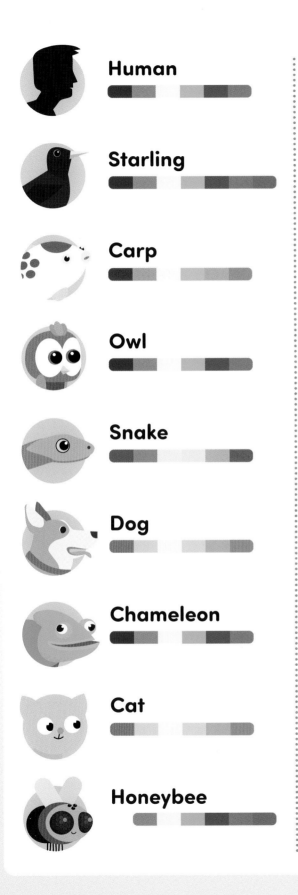

Human

Starling

Carp

Owl

Snake

Dog

Chameleon

Cat

Honeybee

The retina receives the image and transforms it into electrical impulses that are carried by the **optic nerve** to the brain. There are two types of **photoreceptors** in the retina: rods and cones. Be careful not to confuse them: the **rods** allow you to perceive the intensity of the light and they are therefore responsible for seeing in **shades of gray**, which allows you to see in the twilight. The **cones** make it possible to **perceive colors**. There are three kinds of cones **red, blue, and green cones**. Most animals do not have red cones at all: **primates**, including **humans**, have them. The ability to distinguish red has evolved in primates as an adaptation to detect conspicuous (reddish) fruits, as primates feed mainly on yellow, orange, and red fruit. How would you know if fruit is already ripe if you can't recognize its color?

Starling

The eyes of most birds are adapted to daylight. But even **diurnal**—meaning daytime—**species** have many **rods in their retina** that **allow them to see in the dark**. It takes quite a long time for a diurnal bird to find its way around in the dark. Your human eyes will grow used to the darkness in about ten minutes, but the starling's eyes take more than an hour.

Starling

Birds' eyes are large and relatively immobile. The strongly **curved cornea** covers a **large spherical lens**. Birds focus by changing the shape of the lens and its distance from the retina. Birds' eyes can focus very quickly too. This is because their iris is made up of transversely striated muscle fibers and the size of the pupil can change literally in the blink of an eye.

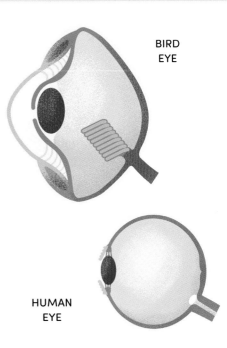

BIRD EYE

HUMAN EYE

STARLING VISION

HUMAN VISION

Birds have a **huge concentration of visual cells in the retina**. They are equipped with cones enabling color vision and rods, thanks to which they perceive changes in light intensity. Unlike humans, they can see the **ultraviolet range of the color spectrum**. A bird that may only seem uninterestingly black to you might be painted in the most beautiful colors for members of its own species.

Do you know which part of the eye has the sharpest vision? It's know as the yellow spot, or macula. Yours has about 160,000 **cells per square** millimeter, while the yellow spot of a **bird of prey** has more than a **million**. Some species even have a yellow spot of various shapes or have several of them! This makes birds the animals with the **greatest visual acuity**.

YELLOW SPOT

Birds can even see well in fog or underwater, thanks to a spectral filter and a protective **nictitating membrane**. Do you know what that is? It's the **third eyelid**, which is transparent, and the birds draw it across the eye for protection.

Take a look at the color of a bird's iris. Most often it's some shade of brown. But the color of the iris changes with age in many species and also **varies between males and females**. Female starlings have, for example, a yellow ring at the edge of their iris, which clearly distinguishes them from males.

MALE STARLING

FEMALE STARLING

Carp

DISTORTED IMAGE

The image that passes through a fish's lens is relatively wide, so its **brain perceives it as slightly distorted**. The fact that the lens is located **outside the center of the eye** also contributes to this. The distance between the lens and the retina is therefore different for different parts of the viewed image. This has its advantages as well. Fish have a sense of what is happening **in front of them and on the sides**. This can be vital to their search for food, and in case of impending danger.

Just like yours, fish eyes are made up of the **cornea, the iris, the pupil, the lens, and the retina**. So how are they different? Firstly, fish have a **rounded and transparent cornea**. This is especially important in the aquatic environment. Unlike air, **water has a similar density to the cornea**, which is why there is not as much refraction of light in a fish's eye as in that of a terrestrial vertebrate's.

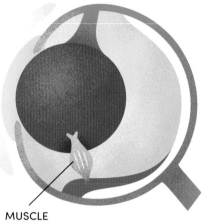

MUSCLE MOVING THE LENS

focus differently: they **change the position of the lens, thus changing the distance between the lens and the retina**. Did you know that a type of photography lens is named after a fish's lens? This so-called **"fisheye"** has a wide-angle lens and can achieve an extreme barrel distortion.

Perhaps the most interesting thing about a fish eye is its **lens**. It is **spherical** and firm, and therefore fish don't focus by changing its shape. Fish, amphibians, and snakes all

WIDE-ANGLE LENS

When a fish looks **forward**, it is **nearsighted**. This means that it can see the image in front of itself clearly and sharply, but it cannot focus the image at a greater distance. The vision to its **sides**, however, is monocular and **far-sighted.** So, they can clearly see what is going on at a greater distance, but cannot see the small prey at their back.

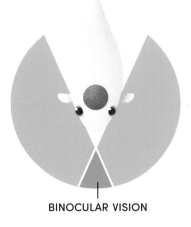

BINOCULAR VISION

Another difference in the fish's eye is that fish **lack both eyelids** and the **tear glands**, which keeps eyes moistened, washes out impurities, and thus **protects the eye from infection**. As they live in an aquatic environment, fish are in no danger of having dry eyes, though. You might be wondering, *How do fish sleep when they do not have eyelids to close? The answer is simple:* **fish do not fall sleep like we do**. They just rest in a quiet place with their eyes open.

The **iris** in your eye functions like a window that **adjusts the size of the pupil**, and therefore the amount of light that enters the eye. In **fish**, however, the **iris** is **inflexible and immobile**, so the pupil is fixed in size. That's why fish take longer to get used to more light.

IMMOBILE IRIS

USEFUL OWLS

European tawny owls have looser **ties with human settlements** and agricultural landscapes than the little owl or the barn owl. But the tawny owl, like all other owls, is a very **useful creature**. It feeds on various rodents, which it flies out to the fields to hunt. It also has a taste for birds, amphibians, and large insects.

Owl eyes are **directly forward facing**. That's why they have **binocular vision**, meaning they can see an object with both eyes simultaneously, just like you. This gives them the ability to judge **height, depth, and distance**. They can determine exactly where the unsuspecting mouse is sitting. The disadvantage, however, is that they have a much **smaller visual field** than other bird

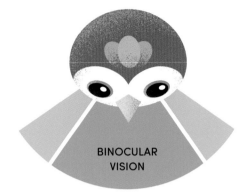

BINOCULAR VISION

species: about 70 degrees of the binocular field, and 20 degrees for each eye.

The owl's eye has one more peculiarity. Their eyes are not held in place in a round orbit, but in a **special ring** which resembles a shortened cylinder. This ring is a bony structure whose purpose is to **protect the eye**. Owl's eyes are so tightly jammed into their sockets that they cannot swivel them inside. That's why an owl **can only look straight forward**. They can, however, rotate their heads 270 degrees because unlike our arteries, theirs will not get trapped if they do so.

Owls have **huge eyes** that catch your attention. There are many birds with eyes that are **larger than their brains**. Did you know that the ratio of eye size to body size in birds is the largest of all vertebrates?

While **human eyes** can process about **20 images per second**, a bird's eyes can process **150**. If an owl were watching a movie, it would see only a set of **still images**. The bird's eye perceives not only quick movements, but also slow movements. The human eye perceives the **stars and the Moon** at a given moment as immobile objects, while the **bird's eye sees them moving slowly**. This is very important for their orientation.

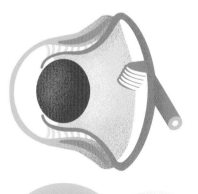

What you imagine to be a bird's eye is, in fact, only a small part of it. Most of the **eye is hidden in the skull**, in a part called the orbit. The visible part of the eye is **highly curved**. The owl's eye has a huge lens that allows the owls to make use of the smallest amount of available light. This is very important for owls, as they are **nocturnal, meaning they come out at night**.

SNAKE EYES

The visual abilities of snakes are associated with their **way of life** and **living conditions**. In particular, **grass snakes** are **diurnal snakes**, for whom sight is an important tool when hunting for food. These snakes have **lenses** in their eyes that **block ultraviolet light** so they can see clearly under bright conditions.

Snake

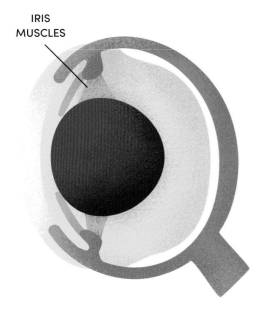

IRIS MUSCLES

The snake's eye is structurally comparable to the eyes of **fish and amphibians**. Their inflexible lens adjusts focus by moving closer or further from the cornea using the **iris muscles**. It gets bigger and pushes the vitreous, resulting in the movement of the lens. The backward movement is then carried out by the weakening of the iris muscles.

PREY DETECTOR

Most snakes have **three types of pigments** in their eye, two of which are found in the cones. In daylight, snakes usually see two basic colors: blue and yellow. The snake's sight is not perfect, as it can only detect objects moving at **close range**. So, when the prey remains still in front of a diurnal snake, the snake cannot see it. However, it will still have its lunch. With great precision, snakes can detect **vibrations** generated, for example, on the surface of the ground. In addition, they have a detector in the form of a **split tongue** that captures and identifies a variety of substances, including **hormones** secreted by the struggling prey.

ROUND PUPIL

VERTICAL PUPIL

Snakes that hunt **during the day** have a **round pupil**. Snakes with a **vertical pupil** adapted to dim light conditions are mostly **nocturnal**. Examples of the latter kind of snakes are boa constrictors and vipers. The vertical pupil allows snakes to regulate the amount of light that enters the eye. When there is a lot of light, the pupil narrows and **protects the retina**.

Some snake species can process **infrared radiation**. The **higher the temperature** of the object, the **more the infrared radiation reflects**. Warm-blooded birds and mammals can be tracked down relatively easily by snakes, despite the light conditions, even in complete darkness. Their heat detectors are not located in the eye but in **special holes on the head**.

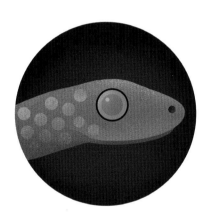

Have you ever seen a snake blink? Probably not. That's because the **eyelids of a snake are fused and transparent**. The membrane covers their eyes and provides protection. This makes it a part of the snake's skin, and therefore the eyelids, together with the old skin, are also **shed**. When you see that the snake's eyes are cloudy, it's time for shedding.

DOGS AND TELEVISION

Have you ever wondered if dogs perceive TV the way we do? Surprisingly, they do. They even have their **own TV channel**, which is tailored to their needs and helps stop them from feeling lonely when their owner is not at home. You will find a ton of dog action on dog TV shows, because dogs prefer things in **motion** rather than static shots, all of course in the shades of popular dog colors. Dogs also like to watch TV from short distance, because of their **nearsightedness**.

Dog

You undoubtedly know that there are a great number of breeds of domestic dog. They can be small or big, hairy or naked, friendly or strict guards. It is surprising how many different breeds evolved from the wild wolf! Dog breeds have always been **bred for some purpose**. In some breeds, mainly **hunting dogs**, the reason for the breeding was to sharpen, as much as possible, the dog's senses.

NIGHT HUNTERS

Wolves mainly hunt at night when it's dark. The only source of light is often the moon and stars. A perfect sense of smell and hearing are the best helpers when hunting, although visual orientation is important for them as well. The light receptors are adapted to this: **dogs have only two types of cones in the retina, but they have many rods**, thanks to which they can distinguish many shades of gray. While their perception of color by cones is limited to shades of **yellow, blue, and black,** the number of rods allows dogs to see well, albeit in **shades of gray**, even when very little light is available.

The extent of the **visual field** in the domestic dog is significantly affected by the **shape of the skull**. The extent of the visual field in dogs with short snouts is smaller than in dogs with longer snouts.

Dog eyes are a bit flatter than ours. Because of this, their **lenses cannot focus as well as ours can**. That's why dogs like to sniff you. Dogs also have a **larger pupil** and their eyes angle slightly to the side. They therefore have **better peripheral vision** and can see you, even if you approach them from the side.

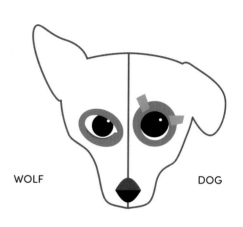

WOLF   DOG

Dog eyes are framed by a **special pair of muscles** that engage when the eyebrows are stretched. With such a look, which is especially well mastered by **puppies**, the owner falls in love with the dog in the same way they might with a **human baby**. Wolves, on the other hand, do not have this ability, which means that it only evolved in **domesticated dogs** to help them bond with their owners.

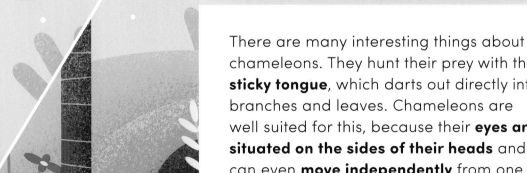

COLORS OF A LIZARD'S WORLD

There are many interesting things about chameleons. They hunt their prey with their **sticky tongue**, which darts out directly into branches and leaves. Chameleons are well suited for this, because their **eyes are situated on the sides of their heads** and can even **move independently** from one another. Chameleons also have a huge field of vision, up to 360 degrees, even partially seeing behind themselves.

Chameleon

Chameleon skin consists of several layers: the upper transparent layer and the other three lower **layers**, each of which **reflects light differently**. Thanks to this, chameleons can mix colors based on their **current mood**. Color therefore plays an important role in **communication**. Chameleons create the most pronounced coloration to scare off their enemies and attract females. This is why they have to be able to reliably **distinguish between colors**.

Independent eye movements give the chameleon the ability to **see in more than one direction** at a time without moving its head. It can literally look to the **left with one eye** and to the **right with the other**. How do they do this? Each eye and eyelid is fused, and they have strong eye muscles as well. Their eye movements are also very fast, preventing their prey from noticing them. **When the chameleon finds its prey, it aims both eyes at it**, judges the distance, and then attacks with absolute precision.

The chameleon has a **curved lens**, also known as a negative lens. It significantly enlarges the image seen on the retina. The chameleon can therefore **increase its visual perception** way more than most animals! The curved cornea contributes to this as well—thanks to it, the chameleon can concentrate light into a **narrow visual field**.

HUMAN LENS

CHAMELEON LENS

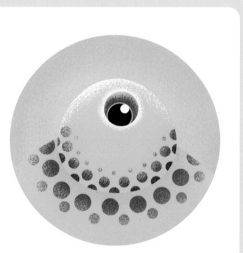

Take a look at how the eyes of a chameleon are placed. It is as if they were hidden in some kind of tower, with only their tips peeking out. These "towers" are made up of **overgrown eyelids**. They are extremely strong and designed **to protect the eyes**.

Lizards, together with snakes, belong to the class of vertebrates called reptiles, but their eyes are slightly different: they are more like those of birds. Unlike snakes, **lizards have movable eyelids and can blink**. Did you know that lizards **get rid of the cornea during shedding**? They do not, however, shed their skin in one piece like snakes, but rather in patches.

Cat's eyes face forward, just like yours. Thanks to this, cats have perfect spatial vision. This allows them to **estimate distances very accurately**. By contrast, the properties of the eye that enable high-quality spatial vision reduce the extent of the visual field, which is a little narrower than that of humans. This, however, is compensated for by greater **head mobility**. Cat's eyes also catch even the slightest movement in grass caused by the presence of prey, clearly distinguishing it from movements caused by the wind.

Another interesting adaptation of cat eyes is the ability to actively **control the amount of light that reaches the eyes**. When a cat is lying **in the sun**, its pupils are retracted into the shape of a **narrow slit**. When the cat is active **at dusk**, in contrast, its pupils occupy almost the **entire surface of the iris**. In addition, the pupil has the shape of a vertical slit, thanks to which the cat's vision has a higher resolution in the horizontal direction. And that's not all! **A cat's pupil has a 50% larger diameter than a human's**.

Every mouse would definitely agree that a cat is a dangerous night hunter. Not only does the **tapetum lucidum**—*a reflective pigment in the eye that makes it shine when illuminated in the dark*—help the cat hunt, but so does the high-quality spatial vision allowed by the **curved cornea** and the **large number of rods**. With such equipment,

the cat does just fine with only starlight even on the darkest night. Do cats see colors? They can see some, their eyes have **some cones** as well. There aren't very many of them, though, and during the day, cats see only **shades of blue and yellow**.

Like many other vertebrate species, cats have developed a **third eyelid** called a **nictitating membrane**. The cat, however, **cannot control it**. The nictitating membrane slides across the eye, for example, when there is an imminent danger.

The eyes of cats are very similar to those of humans. Its structure differs, however, in terms of the presence of special cells located behind the retina. These cells form a special **reflective layer** in the cat's eye, scientifically called *tapetum lucidum*. You can see it at night when the **eyes of cats are green**. Light consequently passes through the eye twice and the cat can see better and much clearer at dusk.

Tapetum lucidum basically works like a mirror. This results in one **negative effect:** the **scattering of the light**, which decreases the resolution of the resulting visual perception. Similarly, **image sharpness** is low due to the low number of cones in the eye. Objects at a distance of more than 20 feet appear blurry to cats and therefore they always **hunt their prey up close**.

A COMPOUND EYE

The eye of an **insect** is made up of many optical elements arranged in a **radial pattern**, called a **compound eye**. Each element contains an inflexible **small lens** with cones beneath allowing for **color vision**. Most insect species have two types of photosensitive substances in their eyes: blue and green pigment, and **insects do not see red at all**. Additionally, bees have a pigment for vision in the **ultraviolet** part of the spectrum.

Honeybee

COMPOUND EYE

EYE UNITS

Each eye unit in the compound eye captures light from a different direction, and **combined they create an image of a wide area**. Since the tubular eye units are arranged in a radial pattern, the insect has a very wide field of vision and—unlike humans—its peripheral vision is as sharp as the dead center of its vision. This is important for insects to rapidly detect approaching predators—or prey—coming from all directions. However, despite its super-sharp peripheral vision, its vision overall is blurry compared with the central vision of the human eye.

The great advantage of a compound eye is the ability to **perceive the light** of the sun or moon when they are hidden **behind the clouds**. If the bees could not see this light, they would be unable to find their way to food or back to their hive. This is also related to insects flying toward **artificial light**. They do this because artificial light strikes each eye differently from the light of a distant moon, which is confusing for insects. It is therefore unsurprising that a confused beetle often rushes to the nearest light source, for example a streetlamp.

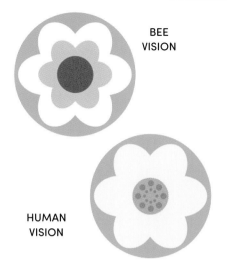

BEE
VISION

HUMAN
VISION

Most bees use **pollen** and **nectar** as food sources. Flowering plants are therefore vital for bees; without them, they would starve to death. And conversely, honeybees are important flower **pollinators**. That's why plants have **different-colored flowers to attract bees**. Even a seemingly inconspicuous flower can have a pronounced color in the ultraviolet spectrum.

THOUSANDS OF EYES

The **small eyes** that make up the compound eye are called *ommatidia*. Their number differs for individual members of the hive. The **queen bee** has the least of them—only 4,000. She spends most of her time in the hive, so sight is not as important to her as it is to the **worker bees**. They have up to **4,500** ommatidia. The big eyes of **male honeybees** are made up of **9,000** tiny lenses.

WORKING BEES

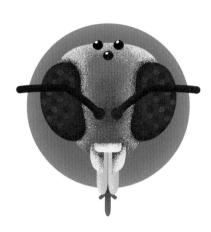

Honeybees are farmed to produce **beeswax**, **bee glue**, and of course **honey**. This, however, is not all that bees do for humankind. Every gardener will tell you how important bees are for **pollinating plants**. In fact, without their industry, most fruit trees and many flowering plants would not get pollinated at all.

© Designed by B4U Publishing for Albatros,
an imprint of Albatros Media Group, 2022.
5. května 22, Prague 4, Czech Republic.
Written by Marie Kotasová Adámková
Illustrated by Tomáš Kopecký
Printed in Czech Republic by TNM Print, s.r.o.

www.albatrosbooks.com

ISBN: 978-80-00-06356-0